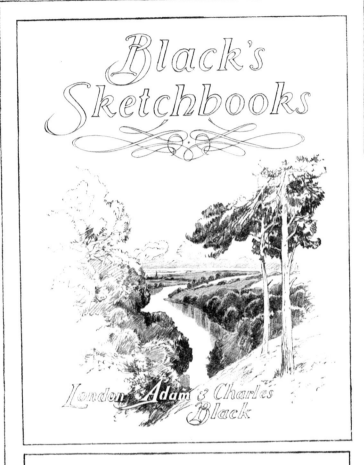

Black's Sketchbooks

London Adam & Charles Black

PUBLISHED B
A. & C. BLACK · SOHO SQUARE

D1439192

EDINBURGH

St. Margaret's Chapel
and Mons Meg,
Edinburgh Castle

A SKETCH-BOOK by GORDON HOME
A. & C. BLACK. LTD SOHO SQUARE LONDON.

Drawings

John Knox's House.
High Street

Edinburgh from
Murrayfield Golf Course

Queen Mary's Bedchamber
Holyrood Palace

Bakehouse Close
Canongate

Gordon
Home

The Canongate Parish Church
and Tolbooth

GORDON
HOME

Edinburgh Castle
from the Grassmarket

[From an etching by J. Houston.

C

The Canongate Tolbooth

Princes Street
looking West

The Castle
from Princes Street
Scots Greys Memorial in Foreground

GORDON
HOME

Edinburgh from the
Calton Hill

Calton Hill

The Calton Hill
seen from beneath
the Salisbury Crags

The Forth Bridge
from Queensferry

First published in Great Britain in 1912
by A&C Black Publishers
36 Soho Square
London W1D 3QY
www.acblack.com

This edition published 2009

© 1912, 2009 A&C Black

ISBN 978-14081-1121-5

A CIP record of this book is available from the British Library

Printed and bound in China